WHAT MAKES A PICASSO A PICASSO?

Richard Mühlberger

The Metropolitan Museum of Art
Viking

NEW YORK

VIKING
First published in 1994 by The Metropolitan Museum of Art, New York, and Viking, a division of Penguin Books USA Inc., 375 Hudson Street, New York, New York 10014, U.S.A. and Penguin Books Canada Ltd., 10 Alcorn Avenue, Toronto, Ontario, Canada M4V 3B2.

Produced by the Department of Special Publications, The Metropolitan Museum of Art
Series Editor: Mary Beth Brewer
Production: Elizabeth Stoneman
Front Cover Design: Marleen Adlerblum
Design: Nai Y. Chang

Library of Congress Cataloging-in-Publication Data
Mühlberger, Richard. What makes a Picasso a Picasso?/Richard Mühlberger. p. cm.
ISBN 0-670-85741-6 (Viking)
ISBN 087099-723-8 (MMA)
1. Picasso, Pablo, 1881–1973. 2. Painting, French—Juvenile literature. 3. Cubism—Juvenile literature. [1. Picasso, Pablo, 1881–1973. 2. Painting, French. 3. Art appreciation.] I. Title.
ND553.P5M78 1994 759.4—dc20 94-18107 CIP AC

10 9 8 7 6 5 4 3 2 1

ILLUSTRATIONS

Unless otherwise noted, all works are by Pablo Picasso and in oil on canvas.

Pages 1 and 2: *Harlequin*, $32^{5}/_{8}$ x $24^{1}/_{8}$ in., 1901, The Metropolitan Museum of Art, Purchase, Mr. and Mrs. John L. Loeb Gift, 1960, 60.87.

Page 6: Man Ray, *Picasso*, gelatin silver print, $13^{3}/_{4}$ x $10^{15}/_{16}$ in., 1933, The Metropolitan Museum of Art, Ford Motor Company Collection, Gift of Ford Motor Company and John C. Waddell, 1987, 1987.1100.18.

Page 7: Brassaï, *Picasso in His Studio*, gelatin silver print, $11^{5}/_{8}$ x $8^{5}/_{8}$ in., 1939, The Metropolitan Museum of Art, Warner Communications Inc. Purchase Fund, 1980, 1980.1023.1.

Page 8: *Self-Portrait*, pen and ink and watercolor on paper, $3^{3}/_{4}$ x $3^{3}/_{8}$ in., 1900, The Metropolitan Museum of Art, Gift of Raymonde Paul, in memory of her brother, C. Michael Paul, 1982, 1982.179.18.

Page 8: *Carles Casagemas*, pen and ink and watercolor on paper, $4^{1}/_{8}$ x $3^{1}/_{8}$ in., 1900, The Metropolitan Museum of Art, Gift of Raymonde Paul, in memory of her brother, C. Michael Paul, 1982, 1982.179.19.

Page 9: *Design for a Poster*, brush and ink, and watercolor on paper, $25^{1}/_{2}$ x $19^{1}/_{2}$ in., 1901, The Metropolitan Museum of Art, Gift of Raymonde Paul, in memory of her brother, C. Michael Paul, 1982, 1982.179.17.

Page 10: *Harlequin*, $32^{5}/_{8}$ x $24^{1}/_{8}$ in., 1901, The Metropolitan Museum of Art, Purchase, Mr. and Mrs. John L. Loeb Gift, 1960, 60.87.

Page 11: *Woman in Green*, pastel on paper, $20^{1}/_{2}$ x $14^{1}/_{8}$ in., The Metropolitan Museum of Art, Purchase, Mr. and Mrs. John L. Loeb Gift, 1961, 61.85.

Page 12: *The Blind Man's Meal*, $37^{1}/_{2}$ x $37^{1}/_{4}$ in., 1903, The Metropolitan Museum of Art, Purchase, Mr. and Mrs. Ira Haupt Gift, 1950, 50.188.

Page 13: *Woman Ironing*, oil on canvas, mounted on wood, $19^{1}/_{2}$ x $10^{1}/_{8}$ in., 1901, The Metropolitan Museum of Art, Alfred Stieglitz Collection, 1949, 49.70.2.

Page 15: *Family of Saltimbanques*, $83^{3}/_{4}$ x $90^{3}/_{8}$ in., 1905, Chester Dale Collection, ©1994 National Gallery of Art, Washington.

Page 16: *The Actor*, $76^{3}/_{8}$ x $44^{1}/_{8}$ in., 1904–1905, The Metropolitan Museum of Art, Gift of Thelma Chrysler Foy, 1952, 52.175.

Page 19: *Gertrude Stein*, $39^{3}/_{8}$ x 32 in., 1906, The Metropolitan Museum of Art, Bequest of Gertrude Stein, 1946, 47.106.

Page 21: *Les Demoiselles d'Avignon*, 96 x 92 in., 1907, The Museum of Modern Art, New York. Acquired through the Lillie P. Bliss Bequest. Photograph © 1994 The Museum of Modern Art, New York.

Page 22: Paul Cézanne, *Bathers*, 15 x $18^{1}/_{8}$ in., The Metropolitan Museum of Art, Bequest of Joan Whitney Payson, 1975, 1976.201.12.

Page 23: Mask, Côte d'Ivoire, Dan, wood, iron, animal skin, cord, $9^{7}/_{8}$ x $6^{3}/_{8}$ in., 19th–20th century, The Metropolitan Museum of Art, Gift of Mr. and Mrs. Bernard Leyden, 1983, 1983.558.

Page 23: Mask, Côte d'Ivoire, Mau, wood, $21^{3}/_{8}$ x 8 in., 19th–20th century, The Metropolitan Museum of Art, Gift of Mr. and Mrs. J. Gordon Douglas III, 1980, 1980.545.4.

Page 25: *Daniel-Henry Kahnweiler*, $39^{5}/_{8}$ x $28^{5}/_{8}$ in., 1910, Gift of Mrs. Gilbert W. Chapman, 1948.561; photograph courtesy of The Art Institute of Chicago.

Page 27: *Standing Female Nude*, charcoal on paper, 19 x $12^{3}/_{8}$ in., 1910, The Metropolitan Museum of Art, Alfred Stieglitz Collection, 49.70.34.

Page 27: *Portrait of Ambroise Vollard*, pencil on paper, $18^{3}/_{8}$ x $12^{5}/_{8}$ in., 1915, The Metropolitan Museum of Art, The Elisha Whittelsey Collection, The Elisha Whittelsey Fund, 1947, 47.140.

Page 28: *Violin and Fruit*, charcoal, colored papers, gouache, painted paper collage, $25^{1}/_{4}$ x $19^{1}/_{2}$ in., 1913, Philadelphia Museum of Art; A. E. Gallatin Collection.

Page 31: *Three Musicians*, 79 x $87^{3}/_{4}$ in., 1921, The Museum of Modern Art, New York. Mrs. Simon Guggenheim Fund. Photograph © 1994 The Museum of Modern Art, New York.

Page 33: *Ornamental Design (Still Life with Guitar and Music)*, color lithograph, $10^{1}/_{2}$ x $8^{1}/_{4}$ in., The Metropolitan Museum of Art, Gift of Paul J. Sachs, 1922, 22.86.6.

Page 33: *Ornamental Design (Pierrot and Harlequin)*, pochoir (stencil), $10^{3}/_{4}$ x $8^{3}/_{8}$ in., The Metropolitan Museum of Art, Gift of Paul J. Sachs, 1922, 22.86.4.

Page 35: *Three Women at the Spring*, $80^{1}/_{4}$ x $68^{1}/_{2}$ in., 1921, The Museum of Modern Art, New York. Gift of Mr. and Mrs. Allan D. Emil. Photograph © 1994 The Museum of Modern Art, New York.

Page 36: *Guernica*, 138 x 308 in., 1937, Museo Nacional Centro de Arte Reina Sofia, Madrid: on permanent loan from the Prado Museum.

Page 41: Peter Paul Rubens, *Horrors of War*, 81 x $135^{7}/_{8}$ in., 1637–38, Palazzo Pitti, Florence; photograph, Scala/Art Resource, New York.

Page 43: *Night Fishing at Antibes*, 81 x 136 in., 1939, The Museum of Modern Art, New York. Mrs. Simon Guggenheim Fund. Photograph © 1994 The Museum of Modern Art, New York.

Page 44: *First Steps*, $51^{1}/_{4}$ x $38^{1}/_{4}$ in., 1943, Yale University Art Gallery, Gift of Stephen C. Clark, B.A. 1903.

Page 45: *Fawn and Starry Night*, 29 x $36^{1}/_{2}$ in., 1955, The Metropolitan Museum of Art, Gift of Joseph H. Hazen, 1970, 1970.305.

Page 46: *Still Life with a Watermelon and Cherries*, linoleum cut (three blocks printed in black, green, blue, red, yellow, brown, and gray), $23^{1}/_{4}$ x 28 in., 1962, The Metropolitan Museum of Art, The Mr. and Mrs. Charles Kramer Collection, Gift of Mr. and Mrs. Charles Kramer, 1979, 1979.620.87.

Page 46: *Squab*, linoleum cut (one block printed in black), $6^{1}/_{4}$ x $7^{7}/_{8}$ in., 1954–55, The Metropolitan Museum of Art, The Mr. and Mrs. Charles Kramer Collection, Gift of Mr. and Mrs. Charles Kramer, 1979, 1979.620.1.

Page 47: © Arnold Newman, *Picasso*, gelatin silver print, $9^{5}/_{8}$ x $7^{3}/_{4}$ in., 1954, The Metropolitan Museum of Art, Gift of the artist, 1959, 59.652.15

Page 49: *Girl Before a Mirror*, 64 x $51^{1}/_{4}$ in., 1932, The Museum of Modern Art, New York. Gift of Mrs. Simon Guggenheim. Photograph © 1994 The Museum of Modern Art, New York.

CONTENTS

Man Ray
PICASSO

Meet Pablo Picasso

This book is about the most famous artist of the twentieth century, Pablo Ruiz Picasso. His imagination was so fruitful that he worked in a number of styles during his lifetime, some of them of his own invention. In his artistic career, which lasted more than seventy-five years, he created thousands of works, not only paintings, but also sculptures, prints, and ceramics, using all kinds of materials. Picasso almost single-handedly created modern art.

The artist was born in a small town in southern Spain in 1881. He began drawing when he was about seven years old. His father was a painter, a drawing teacher, and curator of the town's museum. His mother encouraged him, too, and he even got support—and practice—from his cousins. They were amazed at how accurately he could draw anything he saw. "Draw that," one of them would yell whenever an animal was near, "and start with the ear," or "start with the right front hoof." Each time it was a new animal and a different starting point, and each time Picasso drew it. In fact, by the time he was a teenager, he could do anything with pencil or paint that his

Brassaï
Picasso in His Studio

father or any of the other art teachers in Spain could do. Recalling how proud his father was of his talent, Picasso said, "He gave me his paints and brushes and he never painted again."

A Fascination for Paris

Picasso lived in quiet provincial towns until he was about fourteen, when his father moved the family to Barcelona, a sophisticated city in northern Spain. There the young artist met many talented painters and writers who were fascinated by new ideas coming from Paris, which was the artistic capital of Europe at the time. Picasso and his friends read everything they could find about

SELF-PORTRAIT
Picasso created self-portraits throughout his life. As a young man, he portrayed himself as more dashing and sophisticated than he really was, labeling this image "Yo," meaning "I."

CARLES CASAGEMAS
Picasso made this series of portraits of the artists and writers who gathered at "Els Quatre Gats," a Barcelona café. Carles Casagemas shared studios with Picasso, first in Barcelona, then in Paris.

the Paris art scene, and they talked about almost nothing else.

Picasso excelled in his studies at the art academies of Barcelona and Madrid, and learned much from looking at the great old master paintings in the Prado, Spain's national museum. But he knew that Spain could add nothing new or modern to his artistic education. When he was nineteen, at the turn of a new century, he left for Paris with his good friend and fellow artist Carles Casagemas. For a few months, they shared a studio in the part of the city where other Spanish artists settled.

Paris became the center of Picasso's career, and he quickly absorbed everything he saw. He spent many days studying the art found in Paris's major museum, the Louvre. The Louvre became his day school, and the cafés, where he met fellow artists as well as musicians, writers, and poets, were his night school. Like other artists working in Paris, Picasso found the city's exciting and colorful nightlife a source of inspiration.

Used to the warm sun of Spain, Picasso was very cold in Paris. The days were often dreary and wet, and he lived and worked in unheated rooms. He frequently caught colds and had to confine himself to bed, covered with as many blankets and garments as he could find. He was miserably poor, even though he had sold some of his paintings at an exhibition of his work. And he discovered that Paris was teeming with people even poorer than himself who were struggling simply to exist. Because he could not afford to buy anything fine for his sparse studio dwelling, he painted life-size pictures on its walls of grand furniture and accessories. But this was just pretending that all was well.

Between 1900 and 1904, Picasso traveled back and forth between Spain and France. In the spring of 1904, he settled permanently in Paris.

DESIGN FOR A POSTER

Harlequin

The white marble tabletop identifies the setting in this painting as one of Paris's many cafés. The man's costume and makeup indicate that he is Harlequin, a traditional circus character. Here he appears not at work, but at rest.

Picasso used the gentle curve of the tabletop throughout his composition. It repeats itself in Harlequin's hip, his upper arms, the fingers of his right hand, and even the shape of his head. The seat back and the bright flowers on the wall have the same gently rounded shape. The movement of these wavelike forms leads to Harlequin's white face and long fingers. The lively ruffles near his collar and his cuffs also draw attention to his large hands and quiet profile. His blue and black checkered costume does not follow the contours of his body, but creates a pleasing pattern against the blue-green booth. Picasso used bold outlines around the figure and the table and vast rounded areas of deep color throughout his painting. He did not show a source of

light, or shadows, which would have created a sense of depth and volume. Instead, he chose deep colors with flecks of brighter ones to capture the atmosphere of a café at night.

The Artist Alone

Color sets the painting's mood. Although Picasso used white, yellow, and red, it is blue that dominates the composition. Here it helps suggest that Harlequin is not happy, even though his role was to bring laughter and joy. Picasso often pictured clowns melancholy and alone rather than performing. Perhaps he identified with them.

The appeal of Paris's exciting nightlife was shattered when Picasso's friend Casagemas committed suicide. In love with a woman who did not love him, the young man shot himself in a café. At about this time, blue increasingly began to dominate Picasso's paintings, and sad clowns became a frequent subject.

WOMAN IN GREEN

In 1901, Picasso used pastels to create this image of a richly costumed woman, who was probably a stage performer. The quickly sketched forms seem light and airy. The deep blues and purples, combined with touches of yellow, create the impression of nightlife.

The Blind Man's Meal

The Blue Period

The years from 1902 to 1905 are called Picasso's Blue Period, because at the time this color dominated his paintings. Like the color, his subjects were sad. In this work, he shows a poor and lonely blind man.

As he had depicted Harlequin, Picasso painted a lone figure seated before a table. Here, though, the sense of solitude and sadness is even greater. The blind man uses his fingertips for eyes. His empty plate and the barren room indicate his poverty. The man's arms form right angles, which ground him to the table. One hand clutches a roll, and the other gropes tentatively for the jug.

Almost everything is in a shade of deep blue-green: the walls, the table, the man's beret, scarf, and shirt, even the napkin and the shadows on his gaunt face. His expression is blank and remote and the scene is stark, ornamented only by the tiny patterns on the dish.

During this period, Picasso often emphasized outlines in his paintings, and his subjects frequently struck angular poses. His distortions of line and color were so unusual that he sold little of what he made.

When Picasso returned to Paris in 1904, he painted his final blue canvases, including *Woman Ironing*. She stands hunched over, pushing her heavy iron. Her face is empty of expression, like her spare surroundings.

Because the characters Picasso created during his Blue Period do not have individual features, they are more than just images of poor Parisians. Picasso makes them into symbols of sadness and loneliness that every human being can understand.

WOMAN IRONING

13

Family of Saltimbanques

Here Picasso pictures six traveling acrobats, or saltimbanques, lost in a barren landscape. Some are dressed as traditional circus characters. The man at far left in the costume of multicolored

triangles is Harlequin. He loves Columbine, the woman in the lower right. The man in red is dressed as the jester, or fool. The little girl is a dancer and the two boys are dressed as tumblers. The older boy carries a drum that he will beat to attract a crowd, although here an audience is nowhere to be seen.

Performers Without an Audience

Picasso's sad figures fill much of the canvas, and the empty space around them gives the impression that they are in an almost endless expanse of desert. Here and there, the artist mixed the color of the sky with the earth tones. The lively marks that represent clouds were done in the same manner, in contrast to the detailed painting of the figures. The result is that the sky and earth seem to be one, and the saltimbanques are out of place in the landscape. They would float if Picasso had not provided a few shadows to hold them to the ground.

This surrounding emptiness reflects the moods of the figures. The little ballerina holds Harlequin's hand, but the others make little contact with each other. Instead, they look away from one another, their eyes blackened in shadow. What should be a happy, lively troupe looks lost and sad.

Family of Saltimbanques was Picasso's first large painting. It is more than six feet high and

THE ACTOR

seven feet long. As the artist developed the composition, he tried out different ideas directly on the canvas.

Under the Spell of the Circus

In his early years in Paris, Picasso recalled, "I was really under the spell of the circus. . . . Sometimes I came three or four nights in one week." He and his friends even befriended the performers they most admired. Circus themes dominated the work he produced from about 1904 to 1906 to such an extent that these years have been called Picasso's Circus Period. It is also known as the Rose Period, named for the color he used most frequently at the time.

Blue and rose are combined in *Family of Saltimbanques*, but the emotional impact of the painting comes less from color than from the way Picasso placed the figures in the bleak landscape. They are close to one another physically, but each is on his own psychologically. Picasso admired the great artistry of the saltimbanques, whose work, like his own, required talent, skill, and courage. To entertain their audiences, they had to stand apart from them. Perhaps that is one reason Picasso showed them so alone.

In the winter of 1904 to 1905, Picasso pictured this rose-costumed actor performing on the stage. On the lower right, a man stands in a box below the footlights to prompt the actor with the next words from the script. Picasso distorted the actor's frame and made him stand out against the dark background to emphasize his exaggerated pose.

Gertrude Stein

Picasso pictured Gertrude Stein sitting with her hands on her lap and looking to the right. Her broad lap, billowing sleeves, and rounded shoulders create a strong triangular shape. The earth colors of her clothes, combined with her pyramidlike shape, make her body look as solid as a mountain. A white scarf, cinched by a rectangular brooch, brings focus to her intelligent face. She leans forward in one direction while looking the other way. Picasso has created the impression that at any moment Stein might shift her weight, but not her penetrating stare.

Picasso's model was very patient, posing eighty or ninety times for this one portrait. She wrote, "Picasso sat very tensely on his chair, with his nose up against the canvas. On a very small palette, which was of a uniform brownish-gray color, he would mix a bit of brownish gray. That was the first of some ninety sittings. . . . Suddenly, one day, Picasso wiped out the whole of the head. 'I can't see you anymore when I look at you,' he told me irritably. . . . Picasso left for Spain. When he got back, he painted the head without having seen me again, then he gave me the picture. I was and still am pleased with my portrait. I think it looks like me."

Painted from the artist's memory and imagination, Stein's face looks different from the other parts of the picture. The features are much more angular, simplified, and abstract than they would be in real life, giving her face a masklike quality. Elsewhere Picasso eliminated many details. The hands have no fingernails or creases, the garment has little texture, and the head is almost as smooth as an egg.

Gertrude Stein was an American writer who moved to Paris from the United States in 1903. She was Picasso's friend and supporter. She encouraged many talented artists, including Picasso, long before they were famous, and amassed a large collection of modern art.

A New Way of Describing

Stein developed a way of expressing herself based on the sounds, rhythms, and repetition of words, rather than on their meaning. Her most famous line is "Rose is a rose is a rose is a rose," which gives a sense of the flower without using descriptive words like "soft" or "lovely." She said that it was the first time in English poetry in one hundred years that "the rose is red." Red is not one of the ten celebrated words she wrote, yet she felt that the color was strongly implied by the others. Picasso must have enjoyed Stein's revolutionary use of words. Like her, he always found new ways to describe familiar things.

Les Demoiselles d'Avignon

Five peculiar figures are pictured here in a topsy-turvy setting, where space and objects are totally distorted. They are the women of the Carrer d'Avinyo, a street in Barcelona. The one on the left seems to be turning into a drape from the hip down. Her body is tinted many earth colors, and the leg that juts forward is outlined in blue. The next two women stare straight out, but their noses are in profile. The ferocious figure on the right has a strangely distorted body. Most peculiar of all is the squatting figure. The back of her torso, the side of her leg, and the front of her face are all shown at once, making it seem as though she has been taken apart and then put together again.

The two women standing on the far left and right pull back a curtain to reveal the scene. The drapery is as stiff as a tree trunk on the left side of the painting, and falls below the frame on the right. More drapes are in between. The drapery mixes up the different areas of the painting and makes it difficult to tell where the figures end and the curtain begins. In the left corner of the canvas, a woman's foot indicates the floor that disappears behind an oddly shattered bowl of fruit. Picasso fractures everything into intersecting pieces.

Nothing in Picasso's earlier work had prepared his contemporaries for this painting. It was unlike anything ever seen before. Although

its subject—a group of nude women—is a traditional one, he transformed it dramatically.

Magical Sources

Picasso found inspiration in the art of many different times and places. Ancient sculpture and art from exotic places were very popular with French artists at this time. This art helped them discover new ways of making images. Picasso had looked closely at ancient sculpture from his native Spain and from Egypt. In 1907, he also saw African masks for the first time. Used in sacred rituals to express magical forces of life and death, they were not meant to represent human features in a natural way, but were symbolic. Picasso once said that *Les Demoiselles d'Avignon* must have come into his mind the day he first saw African art. The painting, he claimed, was his first "exorcist" work—an image meant to drive away evil spirits. He gave two of the women in his composition the features of African masks.

Picasso also looked for inspiration to the paintings of the nineteenth-century master Paul Cézanne. Cézanne had studied nature endlessly, looking for such basic geometric forms as cones, spheres, and cylinders in everything he saw. Years later, Picasso said that Cézanne "was my one and only master." The angular

Paul Cézanne
BATHERS

Picasso greatly admired the work of Paul Cézanne, who died in 1906. Cézanne's paintings of bathers were one of Picasso's many sources of inspiration for his Demoiselles, *especially the way the figures pose with their arms over their heads.*

Seeing African masks in an ethnographic museum in Paris was a revelation to Picasso. He realized that master carvers of cultures he knew nothing about divided forms into triangular shapes, just as he did. Although he was nearly finished painting Les Demoiselles d'Avignon, *he decided to use masks as inspiration for the faces on two of the figures in his painting.*

forms in *Les Demoiselles* resemble those in works by Cézanne.

During the eighteen months that Picasso worked on *Les Demoiselles d'Avignon*, he allowed no one to see it. Thirty-one sketches survive to prove that he worried over every angle in the complicated composition. When he showed the painting to his friends, they were shocked. They had never before seen such wild distortions of the human form or of space. One visitor to his studio said that the picture "seemed to all of us something crazy or monstrous." Another said, "It's a revolution." It was impossible for them to understand it, so Picasso put it away for many years. In the meantime, he did not stop inventing new ways to show traditional subjects.

Daniel-Henry Kahnweiler

This composition of tan and gray squares and triangles is a portrait of the art dealer Daniel-Henry Kahnweiler, who was Picasso's friend and one of the first to appreciate *Les Demoiselles d'Avignon*. In designing this painting, Picasso centered his subject's head near the top of the composition, covering the forehead with a transparent rectangle. Under it are Kahnweiler's downcast eyes, his nose, and two curved lines that look like a pencil-thin mustache. Other details are lost in the shifting segments of suit and shirt, until we get to the bottom of the picture, where the subject's folded hands are depicted as tan shapes with gray lines that indicate fingers. In the dark gray oval between the head and the hands, shirt cuffs and sleeves and a gold chain and pocket watch are visible.

Picasso used lights and darks to make the flat surfaces of his composition move in and out. Every detail is carefully painted with small brushstrokes, creating an interesting texture. It is easy to forget to search for hands, hair, or a familiar backdrop, and simply to enjoy the painting. Picasso once said that the forms in his abstract paintings were there to live their own lives.

This new way of painting was not Picasso's alone; he developed it while working with his friend Georges Braque. Picasso and Braque further explored Cézanne's principle of reducing the visual world to basic forms. Everything they painted was carefully analyzed first to find facets and planes that suggested an underlying structure. They wanted their paintings to show how these basic forms make up what we see. They also showed things from many angles at the same time. A writer looking at Braque's work thought he made everything look like cubes, so he called the new style Cubism. Soon other artists took up the style, and it became popular in many countries around the world.

Picasso thoroughly analyzed Kahnweiler's figure as he painted him, trying to see all of the surfaces that made up his face and head. Equally important were the triangular surfaces of the sleeves and shirtfront. Once he discovered the structure, he took it apart and then rearranged each segment.

Picasso portrayed just enough of Kahnweiler's appearance to convey his individual features. He reduced each part of his subject to its most basic shape, showing these parts from a number of angles at one time. Despite this abstract approach, Picasso was able to capture Kahnweiler's attitude and expression. Cubism was only one of Picasso's many ways of painting, but it was a revolutionary one.

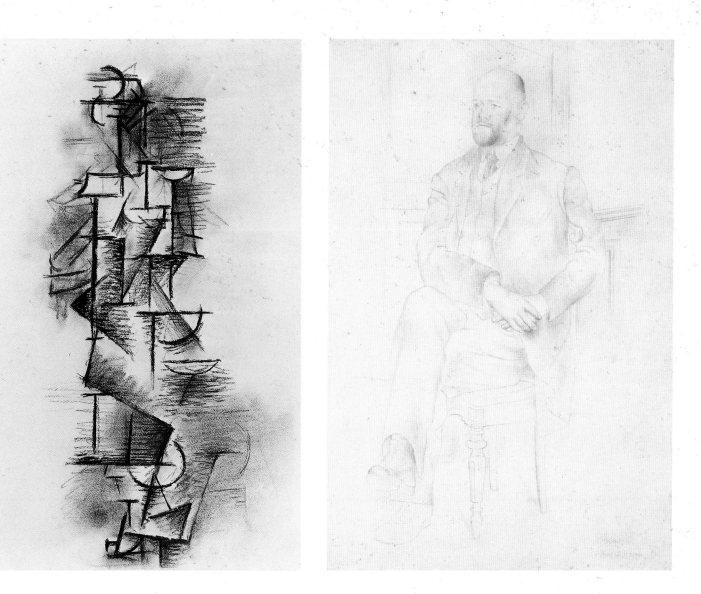

STANDING FEMALE NUDE   PORTRAIT OF AMBROISE VOLLARD

*These two drawings by Picasso, done only five years apart, reveal his wide range of styles. In
the drawing of the nude, he uses straight lines and arcs to capture the structure of the woman.
In his portrait of Vollard, Picasso sensitively describes the sitter's outer character.*

Violin and Fruit

This painting asks the question, "What is real in art? Really real?" Picasso was not the first artist to confuse painted things with real ones. Fooling the eye has been a game of painters since the days of the ancient Greeks. In the painting style called trompe-l'oeil, a French term meaning "deceive the eye," the artist reproduces something so convincingly that it looks like something real, not like a painting. Picasso created reality (and questions about it) not just with paint, but with charcoal, colored papers, old illustrations, newspaper pages, and glue. In doing so, he and his colleague Braque invented a new art form called collage (from *coller*, a French word meaning "to glue"). By using real bits of everyday objects in their works, Picasso and Braque further extended what painting could be.

Modern Still-Life Painting

In the center of the painting appears the fractured form of a violin made of blue paper, brown paper painted with a wood grain pattern, and charcoal drawing on paper and newsprint. To the right, Picasso drew a stemmed glass on pieces of overlapping newspaper. Below it, the title of a newspaper on the table is indicated by the letters URNAL, which were cut off the top of a real newspaper. (*Journal* is the French word for "newspaper.") Picasso also glued down the paper's

sports and financial pages. Because newspapers are flat, he rounded one edge and scribbled shading on it with charcoal to add depth to the composition. In the upper left, apples and a pear are arranged in a bowl made of a semicircle of newsprint. The pieces of fruit have numbers beneath them, because Picasso cut them out from botanical prints. In the lower left, the back of a chair is created with vertical and horizontal brown stripes painted on pieces of paper. By mixing actual objects with painting and drawing, Picasso transformed traditional still-life painting into something very modern.

Newsprint browns with age, so the colors of Picasso's collage are not the same as they were in 1913 when he made it. Originally the colors contrasted strongly with the wood of the violin; now they match them.

Three Musicians

Picasso paints three musicians made of flat, brightly colored, abstract shapes in a shallow, boxlike room. On the left is a clarinet player, in the middle a guitar player, and on the right a singer holding sheets of music. They are dressed as familiar figures: Pierrot, wearing a blue and white suit; Harlequin, in an orange and yellow diamond-patterned costume; and, at right, a friar in a black robe. In front of Pierrot stands a table with a pipe and other objects, while beneath him is a dog, whose belly, legs, and tail peep out behind the musician's legs.

Like the boxy brown stage on which the three musicians perform, everything in this painting is made up of flat shapes. Behind each musician, the light brown floor is in a different place, extending much farther toward the left than the right. Framing the picture, the floor and the flat walls make the room lopsided, but the musicians seem steady.

Music Makers in Harmony
It is hard to tell where one musician starts and another stops, because the shapes that create

them intersect and overlap, as if they were paper cutouts. Pierrot, the figure in blue and white, holds a clarinet in his hands; one hand is connected to a long, thin, black arm, while the other hand lacks an arm. Two brown rectangles between Pierrot's legs and arms represent a table seen from the side, upended and partly in front of the figures, partly under them. As in his Cubist paintings, Picasso liked to show more than one viewpoint at the same time.

Pierrot's blue costume extends to form a mask over Harlequin's face, and the brown wall merges with Harlequin's features. His hands, which are even smaller than those of the horn player, hover near the guitar.

Picasso indicated Harlequin's face as a net-patterned shape and the friar's beard as a wavy-patterned shape. Both motifs were painted to resemble the patterned paper Picasso used in his collages. The sheet of music the friar holds is partly covered by the same blue Picasso used for Pierrot, giving balance to the composition.

The dog is easy to miss for he is painted brown against brown, lying on the floor under the musicians, his tail between Harlequin's orange and yellow legs. The dog's forepaws project almost to the left edge of the painting but, higher up, just at the horn player's elbow, the animal's open muzzle and alert ears appear—far away from his body! The dog may be the inspiration for the pawlike hands Picasso used for all three of his musician figures.

Three Musicians emphasizes lively colors, angular shapes, and flat patterns. Picasso said he was delighted when "Gertrude Stein joyfully announced . . . that she had at last understood what . . . the three musicians was meant to be. It was a still life!"

Picasso painted *Three Musicians* in 1921. By now, Picasso was a famous artist. He befriended and collaborated with writers and performing artists, illustrating books and designing stage sets for operas and ballets.

STILL LIFE WITH GUITAR AND MUSIC
Musical instruments often appear in Picasso's art. This still life is in the same style as Three Musicians.

PIERROT AND HARLEQUIN
As in Three Musicians, *lively and colorful shapes merge into one another, unifying the figures. At the same time, the jaunty hats and firmly planted feet are distinct. Picasso is no longer preoccupied with the loneliness of clowns, but captures their joyful playfulness.*

A book was even written about Picasso's art in 1921. Still, despite his fame, Picasso's art was controversial because it challenged people's ideas about what art could be. Picasso continued to challenge himself, too, and found new inspiration in the art of the ancient Mediterranean world.

Three Women at the Spring

Picasso painted this picture in 1921, the same year he painted *Three Musicians*, but how different the two works are! Three women gather together around a spring to collect water, which quietly trickles from a rock and is guided into a slender ceramic jug. The soft splashing sound of water seems to set this painting's quiet mood. The gestures of the women are as restrained as the colors around them.

The figures crowd the canvas, their hands meeting at the center. The women's physical closeness seems to portray outwardly the trust they have in one another. By making them almost as large as the canvas, Picasso gave them the quality of monumentality, a sense of grandeur. The women's features are rounded and simplified, with heavy outlines and deep shadows. The figures seem as weighty as the rocks they rest on.

This style of work is called neoclassical, meaning that the artist was inspired by classical sculptures from ancient Greece and Rome and made them new (*neo*) through his unique vision of them. Classical statues were admired for their slender, elegant proportions, but Picasso's figures do not share those features. The broad bodies, thick limbs, and squat fingers and toes of Picasso's three women may lack traditional classical elegance, but their long, straight noses, balanced poses, and strength make them resemble ancient statues. The costumes the three women wear are simple, falling in folds like the grooves in the columns of ancient temples.

Picasso said late in his life that he had always loved classical art. He found inspiration in it throughout his career. At the same time, he turned his back on the notion that beauty can be taught by copying classical art. He declared that "training in beauty is a sham." To him, beauty came from "instinct and brain." It had to be original for each generation.

The painting's subject is traditional. A well or spring is a symbol for the source of knowledge and civilization, as well as eternal life. It was the task of women to fetch water for their households' daily needs. At the spring they met other women, exchanged news, and found kinship in their life-giving work. How different a way of presenting women than the way Picasso showed them in *Les Demoiselles d'Avignon*!

Picasso once insisted that "different subjects require a different mode of expression." Cubism and collage were innovations, but neoclassicism was very traditional. Yet Picasso created a neoclassical style that was both personal and unique.

Guernica

Picasso's magnificent and deeply troubling painting about the suffering of war is painted entirely in shades of gray. Dangling high up in the middle of the crowded composition is a naked light bulb, set in an eye shape, sending out spiky rays. Near it, a kerosene lamp is held by a hand at the end of an impossibly long arm. The arm stretches out from a window on the right side of the painting, and the hand and arm belong to a frightened woman who looks ahead and gasps in horror.

Behind the window, a house is engulfed in flames. Inside, a body reaches upward in agony, struck by collapsing timbers. In the lower right corner, a woman escapes the inferno. As she drags herself away from the fire, she looks up pleadingly. Her head and body are both distorted, suggesting the injuries she has suffered.

Near the center, a horse rears and neighs in pain as a lance pierces its body. To convey the animal's agony, Picasso exaggerated its features, depicting it with flared nostrils and a pointed tongue in its screaming mouth. The horse's rider has fallen, landing across one of the horse's hoofs. His left arm reaches out toward the left side of the canvas. His body seems chopped into bits; a severed arm holding a broken sword appears in the bottom center. Above the dead man, Picasso painted a woman wailing in grief, holding her lifeless child. Behind her is a threatening bull.

An actual event drove Picasso to create this painting. While World War II was brewing in Europe, in 1937 the French government organized a Universal Exposition intended to ease the tension. Entitled "Progress and Peace," it was to be held at the base of the Eiffel Tower, and fifty-two countries were invited to display their art. In January of 1937, the Spanish Republic asked Picasso to create something special for the occasion, and he accepted. While he was thinking of an appropriate subject, word came of a tragedy in his homeland. A civil war was being fought there. General Francisco Franco led the insurgent forces against the Spanish Republic. In response to his request, German planes bombed the small town of Guernica in northern Spain. Guernica was the ancient capital of the proud and independent Basques. Although the small city was defenseless, the planes passed over again and again, dropping bombs.

Picasso learned about the brutal attack in the newspaper, where he read that the bombing lasted for hours, killing sixteen hundred people, wounding thousands more, and devastating the city. The artist decided to make this event the

subject of his painting for the Exposition. To develop his idea, Picasso made more than one hundred drawings. He looked at great paintings showing classical and biblical scenes of war, and created something totally new. He decided that instead of showing the actual town, he would use a few representative figures, placing them on a canvas more than ten feet high and twenty-five feet long. In six weeks, Picasso completed the mural, which he named *Guernica*. Through exaggerated poses and expressions, jagged shapes and lines, Picasso captured the frenzied horror of the attack.

Picasso stretched and skewed human shapes to suggest the torment and agony of the women of Guernica. He painted them in profile so their contorted mouths can convey their inner pain and horror. The wailing women express personal grief, while the other two, whose heads are shaped like ghosts, seem to represent the world, asking "Why?"

Universal Meaning

Many consider *Guernica* Picasso's greatest work because it is really about all wars and all cruelty, not just about one day in northern Spain. The characters in the painting refer to symbols that Picasso knew his audience would recognize. The woman holding the dead child suggests the figure of the Virgin Mary mourning over her son's crucified body. The bull, a national symbol of Spain, may indicate that it was a Spaniard who ordered the attack on Guernica. "The bull represents brutality, the horse the people," Picasso explained. The woman holding the lamp is a traditional symbol of justice. But in the end, Picasso said, "It's up to the public to see what it wants to see."

Guernica instantly became a symbol of Spain's plight. When General Franco became the dictator of Spain, Picasso swore not to step on Spanish soil as long as the general was in power. Nor would he allow *Guernica* to be exhibited in his homeland while Franco ruled. Only after Franco's death in 1975 was the painting moved to Madrid, Spain's capital.

Peter Paul Rubens
Horrors of War

Three hundred years before Picasso painted Guernica, *Peter Paul Rubens painted* Horrors of War. *It was one of the many sources that Picasso turned to as he planned his work. Picasso used similar poses in Guernica, and he borrowed the figure of the woman holding a lamp.*

Night Fishing at Antibes

Two fishermen peer at their prey from a round-bottomed boat bobbing in the slow-moving waters of a harbor. One of them is about to spear a fat ocean creature shaped like a whale. The other has unsuccessfully tried to spike a fish, which swims away from him. Picasso painted a whimsical crab in the lower left corner of his picture, putting two eyes on one side of its head.

Just two years after *Guernica*, Picasso painted this very large, mural-size painting in a very different mood. He spent the summer of 1939 in Antibes, a seaside resort on the Mediterranean coast of France. Taking an evening walk along the shore, he was enchanted by the sight of fishermen in boats using large gas lamps to attract their catch. He decided to paint a scene of night fishing.

Picasso used a variety of dark but glowing colors to give the impression of a night scene. He made the fishermen deep blue and the water green-blue, and he represented the torches with yellow and pale green triangles framed in lines extending into the night. Everything glows like stained glass. The largest light is a swirling moon with squared rays, a delightful effect that stains the sky deep red.

Playful Abstraction

The intense green-colored rampart on the right supports the jetty, where the artist's friends stand. A woman holds her bicycle with one hand while lifting an ice cream cone to her mouth. Her friend, enthralled by the glittering scene, stands on her toes and reaches out into the night. Picasso does not emphasize the violence of the men spearing fish. He could use abstract, jagged shapes to capture any subject or mood, and here the mood is playful.

In the background at left appear purple shapes that represent the actual palace Picasso used for a studio. Now the building serves as the Musée Picasso and is filled with the lively works of art he created in Antibes.

First Steps

Using abstract shapes, Picasso shows how difficult it is for a little child to stay balanced and move one foot forward, then the other. The child's twisted face suggests that she must concentrate carefully. She looks straight ahead as her mother holds her hands and slowly releases her grip, freeing the child.

Picasso focuses very closely on the two figures, especially the child, who takes up a great amount of space on the canvas. Only a plain floor and wall appear in the background, and Picasso uses few colors, just as in his earlier paintings. Nothing distracts from the action.

First Steps Are Giant Steps

Although Picasso used abstract shapes to show the two figures, all of their parts can still be recognized. He flattens the mother's face to show her bending over. Her rounded shoulders frame the child, suggesting maternal love and care. In contrast to the mother's round, smooth form, the child is made of jagged shapes, suggesting the energy with which she begins to walk. By making the child grand in scale, but a little unsteady, Picasso shows that no matter how awkward, every child's first steps are monumental.

First Steps was painted in a style that was as familiar to Picasso as his own handwriting.

Perhaps he had forgotten how foreign it looked to people who had never before seen his work. When World War II ended in France, his works were exhibited in Paris. Students violently protested Picasso's style. It was new to them,

FAWN AND STARRY NIGHT

even though two or three generations of art lovers had already learned to appreciate it.

During the last three decades of Picasso's life, his energies went into mastering techniques that were new to him. When he learned to make ceramics in 1947, he produced more than two thousand pieces in one year. He devoted almost all of 1950 and part of every other year to sculpture. Printmaking was another special interest. He produced lithographs, linocuts, and engravings in large numbers. In just seven months in 1968, when he was eighty-seven years old, he made 347 engravings. In these later years, Picasso also painted personal renditions of masterpieces by Rembrandt, Velázquez, and other old masters. He died on April 8, 1973, at the age of ninety-one.

The Modern Old Master

Thousands of works by Picasso—paintings, sculptures, prints, drawings, and ceramics—are exhibited in museums all over the world, making him the best known of all modern artists. Picasso changed art more profoundly than any other artist of the twentieth century. His work gave new importance to personal feelings, to the great events of our time, and to the little things all around us.

STILL LIFE WITH A WATERMELON AND CHERRIES

SQUAB

46

Picasso

Arnold Newman
PICASSO

What Makes a Picasso

Picasso invented new ways of picturing things.
He worked in a number of styles.

Picasso showed objects from many viewpoints at a time, often combining a straight-on view with a profile.

Exaggerated and distorted shapes and colors convey emotion.

Picasso often simplified the things he saw into basic shapes, such as circles and triangles.

Picasso used bold black outlines, sometimes with bright colors.